I am learning all the tir

MW00934617

—
v

Introduction

The inspiration for *You Can Teach an Old Bitch New Tricks* came from my sister Lyn. She loved to ride rollercoasters. She parachuted at the age of 70. I declined those adventures but together we flew over Sedona, Arizona to feel the convergent zones, and had our auras photographed. We sledded down sand dunes at White Sands National Monument. She phoned from an emergency helicopter taking her to the hospital to describe the amazing sight below of lava beds.

We exchanged stories of new learning experiences for several years. She lived in New Mexico and I live on Whidbey Island in Washington, and we talked every Monday by phone. She encouraged me to capture our adventures in poems and this book is the result.

In memory of Lyn Brooks who passed away in 2015 at the age of 84.

A Poem for My Sister after Our Adventure at White Sands National Park

White sand collects sun
and warms our aging bodies

footprints crumble and fade
as we ascend the highest dune

crystals shimmer in the wind
crest into new waves

shadow of a raven
glides across our path

we descend on orange saucers
not the rollercoaster of our youth

will our passage
leave a lasting trail?

we tell stories
of our children and grandchildren

captured granules
pour from our shoes

The Old Bitch

A Piece of Work

A piece of work can be a difficult person
or a work of art.

I began with a malleable lump of clay
that had been pummeled and pinched
into an unrecognizable shape by untrained
but well-meaning artisans.

I took the lump into my own hands
and sculpted an original creation.
There were flaws and imperfections
but they added to its character.

I fired it at temperatures
that allow it to go from freezing
to blazing hot without cracking.

I believe I created a work of art.

A Woman of Few Words

Raised on the fatherly advice
It is better to keep your mouth shut
and be thought a fool than to open it
and remove all doubt,
I am slow voice my opinion.

In addition, I am an introvert.
While I plan my contribution
to a conversation, I rarely find
a place to insert it before I forget.

I make my point quickly
so I won't bore my listeners.
I harbor a secret admiration for those
who are unaware they bore their listeners.

I express myself in poetry.
My poems never exceed one page
after I remove extraneous words
and edit out all adjectives.
.
I am also fond of the seventeen syllables
of haiku.

My History of God

A ghostly presence when I laid me down to sleep
I prayed He would take my soul if I should die before I woke.

Friends who enjoyed a personal relationship with Him
tried to save my soul by inviting me to Sunday school.

I felt His power of damnation when I sipped grape juice
and my friend whispered, *No! You don't belong!*

I was terrified by His presence
in an erupting volcano in a Pathe newsreel.

At Episcopal Youth Camp
He was referenced as a safeguard to my virginity

My father, an atheist, would not let Him in the house.

I might have met Him if I had been saved.

He might have heard me if I had sung in a choir.

I finally made His acquaintance when I was 80
and had a good long talk with a giant cedar tree.

Another Chapter

A Villanelle

I do not feel it so much – old age.
It is just another chapter in my life.
I did not notice when I turned a page.

Don't dwell in the past is a wise adage.
Don't look back – think of Lot's wife.
I do not feel it so much – old age.

I gained some wisdom, not quite a sage.
I skated through without much strife
so I did not notice when I turned a page.

I carefully picked my battles to wage
although the opportunities were rife.
That's why I do not feel it so much – old age.

There is a new play every day on the stage,
a chance to dance to fiddle and fife.
I do not feel it so much – old age.
I do not notice when I turn a page.

Metamorphosis

I travel light, as light,
That is, as a woman can travel who will
Still carry her body around because
Of its sentimental value.
            Paraphrase from The Lady's Not for Burning by Christopher Fry

My possessions form a casing
gathered to protect me.
My belongings weave a cable
that ties me to the earth.

I peel off layers –
clothes to Goodwill
detritus to the dump
Kodak slides reduced to one DVD,
treasures recycled as gifts.

A butterfly can't flit
if it hangs on to its cocoon.

Dancing Solo

Like a toy boat abandoned in a bathtub
up against a cold wall, it feels lonely at first.

Then you bob a little and discover
you can go forward as well as backward.

You can turn left or right on your own volition.
You are no longer restricted to a dance floor.

You are not fragmented in a mirror ball.
You dance to songs you make up.

And if there is no music you dance to bird song
wind in the trees, pebbles pulled by the tide.

I Tell Everyone it's My Birthday

You can call me or text me or love me on Facebook.
You can surprise me with a sweet card in the mail.

You might Tweet, if you know how, *#greatday*
or send a telegram if Western Union still exists.

You could hire a plane with a Happy Birthday banner
and fly over the yacht you have chartered for me.

Please, no *You're how old? Damn.* cards,
no black balloons or a bonfire on my cake.

I flew in a Goodyear blimp on my 75th
and starred at a gala in my honor on my $80^{th.}$

This is not a milestone year, just an ordinary 85th
(June 8, it's a Thursday) so please don't make a fuss.

I will act surprised when a male stripper appears at my door.

The Kind of Friend to Have

You keep your head
when all about you are losing theirs.
You don't seem to realize
the seriousness of the situation,
You are illogically optimistic
and have been called a Pollyanna.

You spend hours on the beach
searching for treasures.
When a double rainbow appears
you stop thinking. Sunlight
on the dew on a spider's web
holds your attention
longer than the evening news.

You find the silver lining of every sad story.
During a driving rainstorm
you exclaim *what a beautiful day*!

You see the good in everyone.
I like hanging out with you.

Beach Bitch

I am windblown and rain-drenched,
an eroded periwinkle.

I hold the key to the keyhole limpet
locked upon a granite rock.

I commiserate with the dire whelk
about moldering algae, red tide.

I hold the gaze of an eagle
who glares at me from atop a dead alder.

The crack of my bull kelp whip
subdues the waves.

I rub shoulders with aggregating anemones.
I wave my feelers, sieve the ocean.

I am a many-tentacled starfish
among blue mussels and razor clams.

It is my face I see in the tide pool.

13

What is Left

I collect driftwood from high water lines,
redwood, big leaf maple,
alder, ancient cedar
remnants of grandeur at the end of their journey.

I carve away everything that is a sign of weakness,
paths sculpted by insects, holes hammered by flickers.

Rings in the wood,
some close together, some widely spaced
reveal years of drought, years of abundance.

Fierce winds snapped branches and sap healed.
Bark hangs on, fiercely protective
even after a long sea voyage

What caused the whorls and nubs, the rot and decay?
What elements played upon a strong trunk,
tenacious roots, veins carrying a life force?

This is what I look for,
the extraneous peeled off layer by layer
and the essential core revealed.

Her Pond

A man's loud voice breaks the silence.
Gadwalls seek shelter
in stands of grey tufted cattails.

He overrides the conversation
of darting swallows trolling for gnats,
the cry of a grackle establishing territory.
He disrupts a blackbird courtship.

He rocks the dock she is sitting on.
Her reflection breaks up.

He blocks the wind raising hairs on her arms.
He asks if he is interrupting.
The old bitch tells him he is.

I Learn To Write It Down Quickly

A random thought is shoved on board
as though by a pusher on a crowded
Japanese commuter train.
At the next stop two thoughts get off.

Synapses sag under the load.
Family stories fall into the creek.
My best friend's name drifts
downstream, around the bend.

I believe it is information overload
rather than diminished mental capacity.
In my 8th decade I create a memory system
that does not involve electronics.

I write it down quickly. That's it.
When I need to retrieve data it's all there,
on to-do lists, scribbled on my crossword puzzle
or on a napkin from my last trip to McDonald's.

Could I Have Been Better?

Harkening back and somewhat curious
was I generous or was I penurious?
Should I have done more or was I just fine?
How much was self-serving, how much benign?

I am a moderately generous person.
I give when asked, because I am not mercen-
ary. I graciously accede to other's demands.
I drop quarters into outstretched hands.

I chair a committee, get out the vote,
drive a friend to the doctor, however remote,
protest wars, bring a casserole,
guide patrons on a gallery stroll.

On review the results might be good or adverse.
I could have been better — but I could have been worse.

Believer
A Pantoum

I believed everything wise men told me,
scientists, thinkers, presidents and clergy.
I remember how ignorant I was, at twenty
at thirty-five, but not today.

Scientists, thinkers, presidents, and clergy
said *a woman's place is in the home.*
At twenty, at thirty-five, but not today
an ivy-covered pedestal had a lovely view.

A woman's place was in the home.
I rode a carousel of endangered species.
An ivy-covered pedestal had a lovely view
of the melting pot that was America.

I rode a carousel of endangered species,
inhaled Chesterfields – *blow some smoke my way* –
swirled in the melting pot of America
when girls were girls and men were men.

Blow some more smoke my way.
I believed everything wise men told me
when girls were girls and men were men
at twenty, at thirty-five, but not today.

Dream Lesson

In *10,000 Dreams Interpreted*
which I purchased today
at the Thrift Shop for one dollar
I learned that a dream of horseradish
foretells pleasant associations
with intellectual and congenial people
and the possibility
of a rise above one's station.

My question is, does it count
if I make a concerted effort
to dream of horseradish
by ingesting some at bedtime?

I already know intellectual
and congenial people
but how exciting it would be
to rise above my station!

But then I might dream
of castor oil which means
I would seek to overthrow a friend
who is jealous of my advancement.

Monkey Mind

At a six day silent meditation retreat
I seek to experience inner stillness.
My monkey mind has other ideas.

She bargains:
if you walk around the circle twice, slowly
you can come in out of the snow.
She argues:
isn't this is a waste of time?
She judges:
that person broke the silence by whispering to a friend.
She criticizes:
you have no friend to break the silence with.
She finds fault:
if the idea is to step out of time,
why did you bring your Timex?
She makes up a story:
that woman is watching you spoon
your soup toward you instead of away.
She amuses herself with lines from old movies:
Here's looking at you, kid.
What a dump!

She finally gives up.
I finish my pumpkin soup,
goat cheese and rice cakes in stillness.

Solitude
A Pantoum

On a stretch of Double Bluff beach
after the erratic and before the downed tree
it is quiet save for the ripple of pebbles.
The beach belongs to me, I like to think.

After the erratic and before the downed tree
under a sky overcast and threatening
the beach belongs to me, I like to think.
No other walkers have made it this far.

Under a sky overcast and threatening
loneliness is an ever hovering presence.
No other walkers have made it this far.
I thought of calling a friend before I set out.

Loneliness is an ever hovering presence
I question my love of solitude
for not calling a friend before I set out.
I can be alone in the company of others.

While I question my love of solitude
I owe it the honor of my full attention.
I can be alone in the company of others.
I invite myself to be my true companion.

I honor loneliness with my full attention
on a deserted stretch of Double Bluff beach
in my own company, my true companion.
It is quiet save for the ripple of pebbles.

One Thing You Can't Teach an Old Bitch

I don't know my right foot from my left.
I say *Oh that left foot* in the tap dance chorus line.
A command to *Allemande right* quashed
my square-dance career.

In yoga class I am the warrior guarding the wrong way.
I torque myself into a twist and face everyone else.

I direct *Turn right* and whoever is driving the car
looks to see which way I am pointing.

I wear a ring on my right hand to tap on the steering wheel.

I transpose enough numbers to suspect dyslexia.
I have a rough time with the Hokie-Pokie.

I know which way I lean politically.
I know I function from a left-brain perspective.

It's just too late to learn my right foot from my left.

The Bitch's World at Eighty

My World at Eighty

This morning I looked out the window
and the horizon appeared tilted.
For one heart-stopping moment,
before panic set in, I was elated.
Today was going to be different.

On TV, BREAKING NEWS
would skew across my screen diagonally.
A renowned earth scientist would lose his footing
as he approached the microphone.

This condition, he would intone,
long known as the Atlas Syndrome,
was observed in ancient Crete
when crows flew into obstacles
they had previously avoided. This was attributed
to the contrary nature of crows.

A list of precautions would appear on my screen:
Secure items on table tops
Wear rubber soled shoes
Stay off beaches
until you determine if the tide is going in or out
Be aware of crow activity

When equilibrium is restored,
a reporter would solemnly announce,
we will resume our regularly scheduled broadcasts
with updates on terrorist activities,
executive actions, unusual weather patterns
and the stock market.

And then my world righted itself. Ah, well.

—

What the Island Teaches Me

Every rise in the road reveals snow-etched mountains.
All roads lead to the sea.

Every beach has secrets to be ferreted out:
a secluded patch of sand, anemones in tide pools,
a lone loon just off-shore, mussels in purple clusters.

From the beach I watch ferries
carrying people halfway coming, halfway going.
I understand why they come but not why they leave.

There is so much to do.
Walk and breathe and pick up a rock.

Connected

I learned to text when I was eighty.
I ask my phone *what time is the Seahawks' game*?
I attempt FaceTime conversations and selfies
but my arm is too short and I look like a fish.

I have a Facebook page and I'm Linked-in.
I do not understand how either one works
but my grandchildren post wonderful photos.
I do not know how to put them into albums.

I play Candy Crush Saga and Spider Solitaire.
I win some, lose some Scrabble games
with friends on my Kindle. I can download books too.
I am considering falling out of a plane in virtual reality.

I synced my I-Phone to Bluetooth in my Prius
so I can listen to podcasts while I drive.
I know how to record my TV shows
and I use the Search function to find new ones.

I have not learned how to follow these directions:
To start a video from the beginning,
tap and drag the circular button (called the playhead)
on the Progress bar all the way to the left.
If your controls disappear during playback,
just tap the screen and they'll reappear.

I have not ruled out Twitter.

Thunder and Enlightenment

Rain pounds on the roof so hard today
I think it could be frogs or fishes.
My daughter swears such things have happened.
I stop meditating and go Google it.

She is right. In the first century AD
Roman naturalist Pliny the Elder
documented just such slithery deluges.
In 1794 French soldiers reported toads.

I would love to have been there in 2010
when spangled perch fell from a dark sky
onto a remote desert town in the outback
and Aussies gathered around the barbecue.

Just now an ominous clap of thunder
could have released tons of frogs or fishes
filling ditches, clogging drains, and sliming roads
before hopping, or in the case of fish, swimming away.

Religious leaders would proclaim the End Times
while scientists cited melting ice caps.
Ecstatic reporters would replay frog footage endlessly.

I hope I don't manifest an inundation of amphibians
by obsessing about them instead of meditating.
But then again, I kind of hope I do.

Beach Lesson

On a lonely stretch of sand
I am intimidated by *Private Beach* signs.
I don't know if they mean
I can walk to some high or low tide line
or if I should walk in the water.

No one asks me to get off the beach
because no one is at home.
The lifeless windows reflect
a water view that cost a lot of money,
a view protected from human flotsam.

The flotsam is safely tucked away
in tents beneath overpasses in the city.
The number of people with two houses
must equal the number of people with none.
I learn I am supposed to walk in the water.

Eight Possible Causes of Vertigo

1. My brain has reached maximum storage capacity
and the sloughing off of data is causing an imbalance
when large chunks are released at one time
such as how to do long division.

2. One side effect of a drug I take for depression is dizziness
which is unfortunate because dizziness depresses me.

3. Blood sloshes into my brain too fast in my yogic practice of
downward facing dog.

4. I attempt to fill out my income tax form.

5. Scientifically, there may be crystals of calcium carbonate
within my inner ear fluid that pull on sensory hair cells
during movement and so stimulate the vestibular nerve
to send positional information to the brain.
In laywoman's words, hairs in my ear tell my brain I'm atilt.

6. I read Leviticus.

7. In a session of cranial massage, a shift in my skull bones
allows some grey matter to ooze into the wrong hemisphere.

8. Or vertigo could just be a by-product of living on a planet
that is sailing around the sun at sixty-nine thousand miles an
hour
and hurtling through space toward the Constellation Hercules
at over forty-three thousand miles an hour.

The Lights Go Out

A wind whips trees and tosses branches
until a blast snaps a trunk that falls across
power lines and blackness descends.

I sit before my darkened computer.
No Facebook, no Scrabble, no emails
to answer, no Ted Talks, no Amazon shopping.

MSNBC is silenced. How much breaking news
will accumulate until the light comes back?
It is a temporary loss of power, like being stalled
in traffic, like anger, like wide awake at 2 a.m.,

like a death in the family.
Until my favorite distractions return
I settle into this already knowing
and wait for the light to be restored.

Selfie

Graduates from South Whidbey high school
point pink rectangles at themselves
and record this exciting milestone.
They show their pictures to each other.
This is not the photo album generation.

My albums line the shelves in my den.
They hold the photographic records
of births and weddings, vacations and sunsets,
family reunions, children and grandchildren.

I hope these 2017 graduates
have a better memory at 80 than I do.

What Counts

It was less than two years ago that I asked
What the hell is an app?

My phone has an app that counts calories
unless I fudge and leave out the fudge.
Another keeps track of the steps I have taken.
I have one that identifies birds
and keeps count of the species I have seen.

What I need is an app to remind me
to give a hug or return a smile.
It would have an electronic ding
to remind me to see an eagle overhead.

This app would keep track of miracles
and count my blessings.
It would count the people I count on.

Poem Written after the Presidential Election of 2016
When I Thought Nothing Could Surprise Me

Well.
Hell.

Plan

I declined to serve on the committee
for Long-Range Planning at church.
I don't even have a long-range plan for myself
other than maybe living to be 100.

At 19 I had a short-term plan
to get married which I accomplished at 20.
I had no plans for children
but I had three anyway by the time I was 26.

I had no career so there was no need
for a blueprint for advancement.
The U.S. Navy made all the plans
about where we would live.

Now I schedule activities on my calendar.
I look at it every day to see what my plan is.
I did make one plan when I turned 80.
I will not serve on any more committees.

How to Remain Optimistic

The Governor is going to fix the roads
and make Seattle's 4,505 homeless comfortable
in tents that don't leak. He has agreed to take in
25 Syrian refugees.

There has not been a bombing in the entire state.
The closest mass shooting was in Mukilteo,
a ferryboat ride away. Climate change actually
works to my advantage with warmer and drier winters.

There will be a $4 a month cost of living increase
in my Social Security and unless there is a coup
I will continue to receive my annuity check.
I have a roof over my head that doesn't leak.

In the shortening days of November
I walk through a carpet of yellow hazelnut leaves.
I feel mist on my cheeks. It must be mist.

What to Do While Julia Cleans My House

I encountered this problem when I gave myself
maid service on my 80th birthday.
It still seems like a good idea
since vacuuming makes my left side ache.
But I am driven from the house by guilt
because I could certainly clean the house myself.

I choose to go to the beach.
It's a beautiful day and Stella is ecstatic.
I come upon a woman watching sand
cascading slowly down a cliff.
We reminisce about an old soap opera
Like sands through the hourglass
so are the days of our lives.

Rounding a glacier erratic
I find a sculpture garden of cairns,
gravity defying stacks of rocks.
What a great balancing act, I think,
to spend hours creating such amazing art
and then to walk away.

Stella comes back from chasing swallows
and putting irritated herons to flight.
My pen runs out of ink as I begin to ruminate
on snowcapped mountains in blue haze.
Julia has probably just gotten to the bathroom.

How to Find My Car

I am embarrassed when I can't remember
what kind of car I drive
to tell the clerk at the garden shop
where to load my Spring annuals.

It is a challenge just to plant these flowers.
In my town there is an epidemic of rabbits
that makes gardening difficult.
But these bunnies are tolerated and even cherished.

I feel I will be tolerated and even cherished
when I cannot find my car.
Someone will take my remote
and light up my Prius and lead me to it.

Lessons From Mary Oliver

The sun has been hiding all day
behind a bank of ever-shifting grey clouds.
Mary Oliver coaxes me out in the late afternoon.

She suggests I look closely.
Daffodils, of course, straggly forsythia
and a split spirea, a casualty of winter winds.
Red madrona bark shimmers in a light mist.

Wood smoke hangs close to the ground
over the neighbor's pink house.
A rusted wheelbarrow is poised for spring clean-up.

Camellias that earlier flaunted their beauty
now pay the price, brown and drooping.
In dark muck pockmarked by deer hooves
skunk cabbages glow in the setting sun.

A returning flock of pine siskins
turns as one and lifts to a top branch.
I scan Saratoga Passage for signs of grey whales.

Mary says, *Spring will slip past if you don't pay attention*.
I hear a call I think is a Barred Owl.
Mary says it is.

Tricks Taught by Birds

When to flock
and when to go it alone.

When to take the point
and when to take a break.

When to sing
and when to raise an alarm.

When to be still
and when to spring into action.

When to migrate
and when to stay put.

When to flap
and when to glide.

When to incubate
and when to get off the nest.

When to be coy
and when to flash a come-hither color.

The Bitch's Poetry

~~Writing a Poem~~ How to Write a Poem

The process, ~~for me,~~ is not one of words ~~bunching up~~
screaming to be thrown ~~onto~~ on the page but rather
~~a probing of memories~~ seeking inspiration and ~~a liberal use of
Google~~
finding the right words to ~~express the feelings that come~~. bring it to
life.

The title ~~usually~~ comes later, ~~after~~ when~~I~~ one sees what ~~I have~~
they have
produced ~~about~~ after a ~~nervous~~ skittish spate of writing.
~~A The memory of~~ A walk in the rain ~~gives~~ might give ~~me fresh~~ one
ammunition
for ~~another~~ a nature poem, ~~greatly influenced by~~ in the style of
Mary Oliver.

~~My~~ If your dog, ~~Stella,~~ ~~accompanies~~ accompanied ~~me and was~~ is
oblivious to the downpour ~~and that seems worth commenting on~~.
~~and so I~~ ~~one~~ you ~~can~~ may write a few lines about her. If ~~I'm~~ one is in
a ~~frivolous~~
lighthearted mood ~~I~~ you may decide to ~~have~~ to rhyme the poem.

~~I search Rhymezone I~~ You can write the first line and then ~~search~~
find a ~~list of~~ word on RhymeZone for the next line.
~~I might read a few Billy Collins poems for inspiration.~~
Line breaks ~~seem to~~ occur naturally but I ~~am conscious~~ one should
be ~~conscious~~ aware
of how the poem looks on the page.

~~I~~ You discover ~~where the poem is going~~ the poem's intent about
halfway through
and ~~at that point I begin to~~ you think about the point~~I~~ you hope to
make.

⏧ You question ~~if it sounds poetic~~ if there are enough poetic ~~turns of~~ phrases to qualify as a poem. Then ⏧ you should put it aside until ⏤you have time to edit it.

How to Be a Real Poet

Real poets major in English Literature.
They wrote poems as children.
They enjoy rare insights and are awarded prizes.
They know what a metaphor is and how to spell it.

Real poets are appointed laureates.
They write every morning.
Real poets always carry a notebook with them.
They are published in literary magazines.

Real poets can follow the rules or break them
because they know what the rules are.
Words flow from real poets effortlessly.
They write poems that no one understands.

Real bitches say *I am a real poet*.

Hard Wrought

My Aunt Nettie would wring her hands
when things got tough. If Mother had a hard day
she said she had been put through the wringer.

When anyone got upset, she would say
don't get your tit caught in the wringer.
She meant the old hand-turned contraption
attached to the washing machine.

She might have said that to me if I cried
when she wrung the neck of a chicken
scheduled for the soup pot. It ran around the yard
without its head just like the old saying.

Once, a poem would gently unwind on the page.
Now I must grab it by the throat and wring out a confession.
It may not tell the truth
but it will say anything to stop the torture.

I learn to kiss goodbye

poets like Shelley and Yeats.
There is not time enough left
to read poems over and over
to unravel metaphorical enigmas.

I kiss being literary goodbye.
Tolstoy, Joyce, and Hugo I could read
but don't want to. I have time
for Mary Higgins Clark and James Patterson

but I kiss mysteries goodbye
so I'll stop fearing a serial killer is lurking
in the mall parking lot, stalking me
from his red 1984 Oldsmobile Cutlass.

Then I would have to kiss my life goodbye
unless someone noticed, waving
and flapping, my pink Playtex bra
poked though a rusty hole in the trunk.

I am not kissing my bra goodbye.

Spider Lessons

I look at the spider on my window.
I wonder if it is the Writing Spider
who might scrawl an inspiration for a poem
or the name of the next person to die.

That is a myth about the next person to die.

There is another myth
that spiders move into houses in winter.
Hobo Spiders do wander in from time to time
looking for a mate, not to avoid the cold.
They trap flies so I tolerate them.

The spiders in my laundry room
are Long-bodied Cellar Spiders.
They spin great looping webs
that get covered in dryer lint and are unsightly
but they also trap a lot of flies.

My Writing Spider is still on the window,
perhaps wondering what is keeping him
from returning to his natural environment.
I watch to see if he writes *help*.

Rite in the Rain

A miniature stream snakes across the page
ferrying a boatload of homeless phrases
in search of a poem –
morbid sky reflected on a rain spattered pond
hunched heron trailing water beads from white feathers
raucous cries and red wing flashes among cattails.

My drenched and patient dog
wants me to put down my pen.
She wants to continue on the path through the woods
with its bounty of traceable smells –
deer curled in flattened bracken
rabbits crouched in anticipation
tantalizing hints of dogs who have gone before.

I want my words to be as numerous
as the recent hatch of mayflies.
I want the dips and sudden shifts
of a swallow in joyful pursuit.
I want my poem to spread in concentric circles
like the aftermath of a rainbow trout.

I close my All-Weather Field Notebook
and set out to make my dog happy.

—

Inspiration

November is *National Write a Novel in a Month*
and authors are encouraged to pen 50,000 words
track their progress, get pep talks
and meet fellow writers online and in person.

I am inspired to write a poem-a-day.
Since my poems rarely exceed one page
or 230 words a day, 6,900 in a month, it will
be easy. I can always resort to haiku.

But it is 3:37 p.m. on the eighth day
and the demons that previously limited
my output to two poems a month have been aroused.
How many ways can I describe a spider's nest?
Full moons, sunsets, the sorry state of the world?
My dog Stella may be captivating only to me.

But I know how to track my progress.
I can give myself a pep talk. I just did.
When I meet my fellow writers I will advise
full moons, spider webs, and Stella are all good.

.

My Bitch

Stella Sees Snow

The first flakes of November drift down
and Stella is oblivious in her grey fur coat.
Her nose to ground, she sniffs each rabbit track.
She stops to take care of business.

Stella looks up. She becomes very still.
The snow doesn't move like a bee. It has no scent.
She doesn't chase it to make it go away.
I let the flakes fall on my face.

Dog Lessons

Stella rouses me at five minutes past six.
She flops her body onto mine
and raises her head to be scratched.

As I perform this ritual I look out the window
at November's dark shadows and dense fog.
I dread the arrival of ever shorter days.

I let her out and Stella clears the yard
of suspected rabbits, deer, birds and coyotes.
Her bark is eager and fearless.
She takes her responsibilities seriously.

She greets my friends with joy.
She naps between encounters.
She does not appear to think about anything.

I decide to learn from her example.
I will take my responsibilities seriously.
I will be fearless.
I will stop thinking.
I will bark when I need to.
I will hug my friends.
I will enjoy my naps.
I will quit bitching about days growing shorter.

How to Take a Walk

I recognize a Northern Harrier
by the white strip on its rump
and a Stellar Jay by it flight pattern.
My backyard birds list is sixty-four
and my life list is over four hundred.

When I was unable to identify
the breed of my rescue dog Stella
it didn't seem so important to name things.
I gave up bird watching for dog walking.

Stella may have a life list of smells
but she approaches each mail-box post
with the excitement of a botanist
discovering a new species.
She doesn't think *hmmm, probably a Corgi.*

Staying Open to the Idea of Reincarnation

My dog is not the reincarnation of my calico cat,
a fantasy of my hairdresser who believes
her two poodles are Mitzi and Franz returning
after years of faithful geeing and hawing.
Yes, they were horses. And yet

it is just a year since my incontinent cat Sadie
piddled for the last time on my persimmon-red rug.
Stella, rescued from the ultimate put-down
is one year old. Ecstatically bounding
into her new home she marks her territory
on that very same rug. Coincidence

perhaps but her coloring, a merle Aussie –
black cheek, patchy brown flank, subtle grey undertones –
is reminiscent of Sadie's multi-colored coat.
My dog's one blue eye is as baleful as the yellow glare
from a cat when asked, please, to get out of my chair.
Perhaps clear-cut personality differences

will manifest. Sadie the cat never came when called
and Stella the dog comes when a rabbit is not calling
louder. But Stella has a strange proclivity
for flushing chickadees, a small bird of interest mostly to cats.

Sadie the cat did not romp on the beach
although she would have enjoyed the dead crabs.

Stella soars over driftwood, chases receding waves,
greets each frolicking dog, jumps on its owner,
careens down sandy cliffs, trots back to see why I'm so slow,
jumps on me. Of course, Stella is not Sadie born-again –
no cat would deign to come back as a dog.

More Inspiration

She comes in with a headshake
that rattles her collar.
She flops at my feet with a sigh.
You have been staring
at that blank Word document
for a long time, she says.
Do you have writers block?
I could use some inspiration, I reply.

How long has it been
since you wrote about me?
I tell her the last one
was how adorable she was
when she looked at her reflection
in a heart-shaped rain puddle.
Before that it was how funny she was
trying to herd swallows.
I could write about
how patient you are, I supposed.

She sprawls next to me
but her eyes are open. She waits.
Maybe we should take a break
and go for a walk, I say.
She jumps up and heads for the door.
Don't take forever putting on your shoes
and coat and getting the poop bag
and finding my leash, she begs.
I'm coming, I say.
Maybe I'll get an idea while we walk.

Dogged

A neighbor's dog is yipping its little head off.
It is frantic.
Perhaps its owners went to work and left it alone
or someone walked past its house.

I begin my daily yipping
to express outrage at the general off-ness
of the world. I too have been left alone.
I too wonder about people walking past my house.

I like the sound of my voice. I yip
until I experience profound insights –
they are not coming back
my bark is not loud enough to scare anyone off
and I curl up by the fire.

Herding Swallows

I watch Stella herd barn swallows.
They swoop low over newly cut grass
all dark blue and rufous, forked tail acting as rudder.

With great speed and a graceful sweep and pivot
Stella charges at them. One by one
they migrate in the direction she wants them to go.

A swallow does an abrupt swerve
in pursuit of an insect and Stella gives chase.
She no sooner turns this rebel than another bolts
and she must bring it back to the flock.

Stella patiently works this field, back and forth,
just for the satisfaction of corralling swallows.
I chase errant images, lose one and go after another
just for the satisfaction of corralling them into a poem.

Making Amends

This morning when I discovered her
asleep on the couch instead of beside me
I feared she harbored a resentment
from a misunderstanding during our walk

the previous evening. It was dark when we set out
but I had a flashlight and I suggested she stay
by my side. Maybe it was the tone of my voice
but she gave me a look of disdain, her one blue eye

able to convey pure malevolence. I may have
spoken too sharply, *heel!* at the moment
she used the excuse of spotting a rabbit
to bolt. She is merle, various shades of grey

and invisible at night. My flashlight beam
caught her but she disappeared under a bush.
I might as well have been whistling Dixie
for all the response I got. There was screaming

and threats, on my part, and wounded silence
on hers. Then she returned all waggy tail
as though nothing had happened.
I hate her passive aggressiveness.

I withheld *good girl* but she hopped into bed
and snuggled next to me. I thought everything
was alright until I saw her on the couch,
I will do my best to earn her forgiveness.

Almost the End

Face It Bitch. You Can't Attend Your Own Funeral

I know, I know, but I've made preparations –
my will, a power of attorney, a green burial site
and a *do not resuscitate* directive taped on my refrigerator door.
I want to hear how resourceful I've been.

I knitted my shroud in my favorite colors
of magenta, teal blue, rust and forest green.
I left the phone number of the weaver
who creates caskets of natural material. I chose bamboo.
I want to hear how creative I was.

My son Jeff and his wife Lilly are learning to play
Morning Has Broken on guitar and piano.
I chose a Mary Oliver poem about sleeping in the forest.
I requested the congregation sing *Bye, Bye, Blackbird*.
I want to hear them.

All my shortcomings will be overlooked.
My faults will be turned into virtues.

I would really like to hear that before I go.

More to Learn

What is the hardest thing you ever did?
Childbirth, standing up to your father,
saying no to your daughter for her own good?

Did you test your physical strength
or defy your inner demons? Did you walk out
on that stage? Did you take the controls and fly?

Do you regret taking the easy path
when the harder way looked too steep?
Do you wonder how your life would be different?

Do you want to speak your truth
but keep asking yourself, Who am I?
What is the hardest thing you will ever do?

Knitting my Shroud

In no hurry to finish I begin to knit my burial shroud.
With wool yarn from a thrift store bargain
I choose purple, a spiritual color, for my head.
Circular needles. Cast on. Knit, knit, knit. No purl.
I cast on too many stitches. Now purple will be at my feet.

A pleasant rhythm emerges and my shroud grows.
I envision the woven bamboo coffin I earmarked
for my children to order. I congratulate myself
on purchasing a green burial plot.

I add the next color, teal green, and drop a stitch.
In an attempt to repair it, I create a small knot
somewhere around my knee. I assure myself
I will never feel it. I hum my funeral songs,

Morning has Broken, Let it be a Dance and Bye, Bye Birdie.
I find I can knit and watch TV at the same time.
Coincidentally *Invasion of the Body Snatchers* comes on.
I watch a few more movies and add burnt orange.

My shroud grows and warms my lap and then my legs.
New colors create an unconventional rainbow.
When I reduce stitches for my head the yarn lumps
and I wonder how I will look in my shroud.

I weave ribbons into the head and foot for drawstrings.
My children ask how they are supposed to fit me in it.
They will figure it out. I have done my part.

Dallas Huth lives on Whidbey Island in Washington with her dog Stella, near her children, grandchildren and great-grandchildren. She attended the Universities of Kentucky, Rhode Island, and Hawaii and got her BA in psychology from Humboldt University in Washington. As the wife of a naval aviator she learned a lot more. At the age of 80, when she sometimes thought she knew it all, she realized she could still learn a few tricks.

Her poetry books include *I Come from Kentucky*, *heart stone haiku* and chapbooks, *Slice of Life* and *Unseasonable Rain*, *Almost a Memoir*. Her poems have been published in the Manzanita Quarterly, Santa Fe Literary Review, Waving, Not Drowning, Harwood Anthology. She received first prize in poetry and in all divisions from the Whidbey Island Writer's Association.

She would like to thank all those who gave her poems thoughtful reading and offered encouragement: Janice O'Mahony, Diane Shiner, Faith Wilder, Mary Goolsby, Jenny McGill, Gina Vander Kam, Emily Day, Jane Klassen, Shera Rose, Hazel Warlaumont and Gail Fleming

43725398R00044